Frogs & Flowers

Impressions of Ponds & Gardens Made Into Quilts

by
Camille Remme

BOYD PUBLISHING

112 -31st Street, P. O. Box 6753
Wheeling, WV 26003

Acknowledgments

All quilts designed, pieced, and quilted by the author.
Photography by James Fraser, Toronto, Ontario.
Graphic Design and Layout by SPPS, 9753 Hampton Court, Fountain Valley, CA 92708.
Printed in Hong Kong.
Second Printing.

Cover Photo: *Frog, Fish, Lilies*

THIS BOOK IS DEDICATED TO
MANY SPECIAL WOMEN
in particular
Jane, Patricia, Susan,
and my mother, Jean.

Table of Contents

Introduction

This book started from one little frog pattern. I was making a quilt and wanted to represent the land, the sea and the sky through strong geometric images. By playing with half square triangle blocks I was able to come up with a good frog block. That was in 1988.

I am still making frog quilts but have found lots of flower blocks to add more interest to these quilts. Flower blocks alone are wonderful design blocks. Since I do not draw or do much applique my geometric shapes are impressions of flowers, fish, and frogs.

Also in 1988, I started taking classes with Mary Ellen Hopkins. These workshops altered my attitude and improved my skills immensely. Neat tricks like corner triangles (see her book, *Connecting Up*) helped me change standard quilt blocks into flower blocks.

Although many patterns are included here, I find that new blocks and new ideas are always evolving. The ultimate goal of most quiltmakers is to create quilts that are uniquely theirs. My wish is that this book may be a catalyst to the creation of very special and personally unique quilts.

CAMILLE REMME
Toronto, 1990

CHAPTER ONE

Getting Ready

About This Book

❖ The instructions and the patterns are aimed at an intermediate level of quiltmaker – one who is already familiar with using a rotary cutter, cutting fabric into strips for use in quilt construction, and who has the ability to look at a pattern drawn up on graph paper and have some sense of what the construction process will be.

❖ In this book all the patterns for the quilts are theoretically based on graph paper with 1 square = 1 inch.

❖ Any measurement may be chosen to equal one square, even a metric measurement. Choosing another measurement will change the size of the finished quilt. You have the freedom to design any size you want.

❖ All diagrams represent finished (sewn) measurements. Therefore, a 1" finished square would use a 1½" cut strip initially. (Assuming you are taking a ¼" seam allowance.)

❖ *NO TEMPLATES* are used for anything in this book and therefore the blocks may look a little rough – so trimming up or cleaning up the individual blocks before putting them into a quilt may be necessary. I must have every size and shape of ruler created and I do find I use them. For each task, the right tool simplifies the process and makes life a lot easier!

❖ Enjoying the way you work is as important as liking the finished product. The process of cutting strips and sewing strips together is a most enjoyable way to make a quilt.

❖ The first frog, fish, and flower quilts I designed (no patterns available) were made by putting various blocks for the frogs, fish, and flowers up on a design wall and moving them around – adding more blocks and enlarging others – until they fit together. The actual sewing together of the blocks was *NOT* easy. By drawing up designs on graph paper first, the construction of the whole top is simplified and the size to make the various blocks in the quilt top becomes obvious.

❖ The border is an easy place to change the size of a quilt. Adding more borders or choosing different borders than the ones shown on a particular quilt is a design element left up to the quilter.

❖ *HAVE FUN!* Remember you are creating not just a quilt block, but also
a *FROG,*
or a *FISH,*
or a *FLOWER.*

Construction Notes

❖ Quarter inch (¼") seam allowances will be assumed for all projects. This is necessary so that blocks will fit together easily. If ¼" seams are not possible when the sewing foot edge and the cut fabric edge are lined up, here is one suggestion. If you have a zig-zag feature on your machine, move the needle a notch to one side by moving the zig-zag nob. Test the seam allowance taken.

❖ Two terminologies can be used when analyzing a given pattern – the *FINISHED* size of a shape, or the *CUT* size of the strip needed to create that finished shape. For example, a *FINISHED* 1" square in a pattern would need a *CUT* 1½" strip to create it. (Remember, ¼" seams are assumed.)

❖ Patterns show only *FINISHED* shapes and measurements. You must add two seam allowances onto all strips when *CUTTING*.

❖ Using and being comfortable with a rotary cutter, and the various rulers made to use with a rotary cutter are important.

❖ When a strip is cut it means from selvage to selvage. You may not use all the strip, so you should have in your sewing area containers of leftover partial strips. I have boxes for 1¼" strips, 1½" strips (the most common size strip I use), 1¾" strips, etc.

❖ Many of the flower blocks would make a great *BORDER* for other quilts. Another container might contain leftover blocks.

❖ When you have chosen a pattern, make all the blocks and put them up on your design wall. Now fill in the background with pieces cut from strips. If the blocks are on a diagonal set you will also need to fill in the edges with half squares (triangles).

❖ Do not start sewing the blocks together yet. Stand back and make sure you like the blocks you have chosen. At this point you could still replace a block or move them around for a more pleasing look.

❖ To sew the top together you need to *GET A GAME PLAN*. The top may go together most easily by sewing the blocks into strips and then sewing the strips together. The quilts with diagonal sets are always made by sewing the blocks (including the end background triangles) into diagonal strips and then sewing the strips together.

❖ Be generous with fabric when filling in around the edges. You can always trim back if there is too much fabric.

❖ Once the quilt top center is sewn together and ironed, even up (square up) the top by adding a strip on each edge for a narrow inner border. Each corner must be a 90° angle and opposite strips must be equidistant from each other.

❖ The narrow border also serves a design purpose. This narrow strip around the quilt top separates the body of the quilt from the outer border (a finished width of ½" to 1" is most pleasing.) This adds a crispness to the final piece.

❖ Borders usually frame the quilt better if they are a little darker than the body of the quilt.

❖ By adding some leaves to a flower block, a rectangular shape may be formed. To form a square, either reverse this process or add strips of background fabric to two sides.

❖ POSTER SIZE QUILTS – Many of the patterns here are what I call poster size quilts – or wallhangings. This size makes up fast, is manageable to sew, and two or three quilts of this size make a wonderful wall grouping (especially on stairways.) Many poster size quilts are created on the diagonal.

❖ If you would like a quilt larger than a poster size, make the appropriate blocks for four small quilts and arrange them so that the four small quilts can later be put together to create a new design.

❖ I work from a stash of fabric. If I want to make red flowers I use many different fabrics, each a bit different, but red in color. I think this makes a pattern more interesting than just one fabric would.

❖ Fabric requirements are not given for the projects in this book. I am assuming that an intermediate quilter can estimate the fabric needed. However, in light of the previous statement, I might use several strips of different red fabrics instead of a single wide strip of one red fabric. Although large amounts of a single background fabric (one to two yards) may be needed, that is not always the case. For example, in *Pastel Gardens*, and other quilts shown, two or more background fabrics are used with very pleasing results.

❖ Some flowers will be explained step by step so that you can see my method of working. I always make more than one flower at a time, and have one sample displayed in front of me so that I can always see what is needed next.

❖ Although you may start with traditional uses of color (e.g. red for flowers and green for leaves), this is not necessary because the images are geometrically strong and do not depend on realistic color choices.

❖ As I work I think of the different parts of the flower I am creating: the center, the petals, the stem, or the leaves.

❖ Although these geometric flowers are only impressions of the real thing, they are beautiful to me. Happy Gardening!

CHAPTER TWO

Flowers & Leaves & Borders

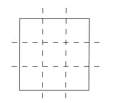

Three by Three Flowers

Based on a grid of 3 squares by 3 squares.
Each square equals one inch finished.
Figure at left shows the breakdown of one block.

Four by Four Flowers

Based on a grid of 4 squares by 4 squares.
Each square equals one inch finished.
Figure at left shows the breakdown of one block.

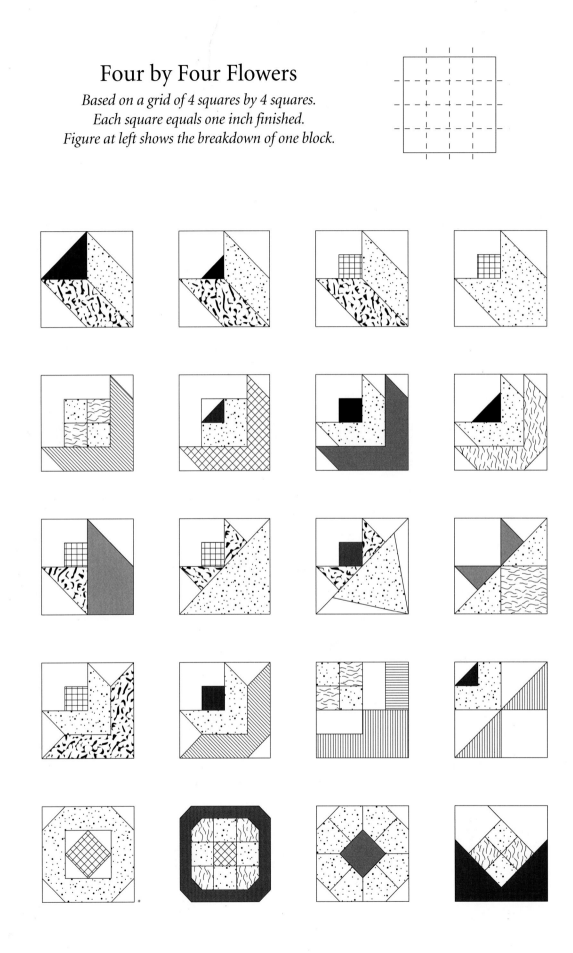

Five by Five Flowers

Based on a grid of 5 squares by 5 squares.
Each square equals one inch finished.
Figure at left shows the breakdown of one block.

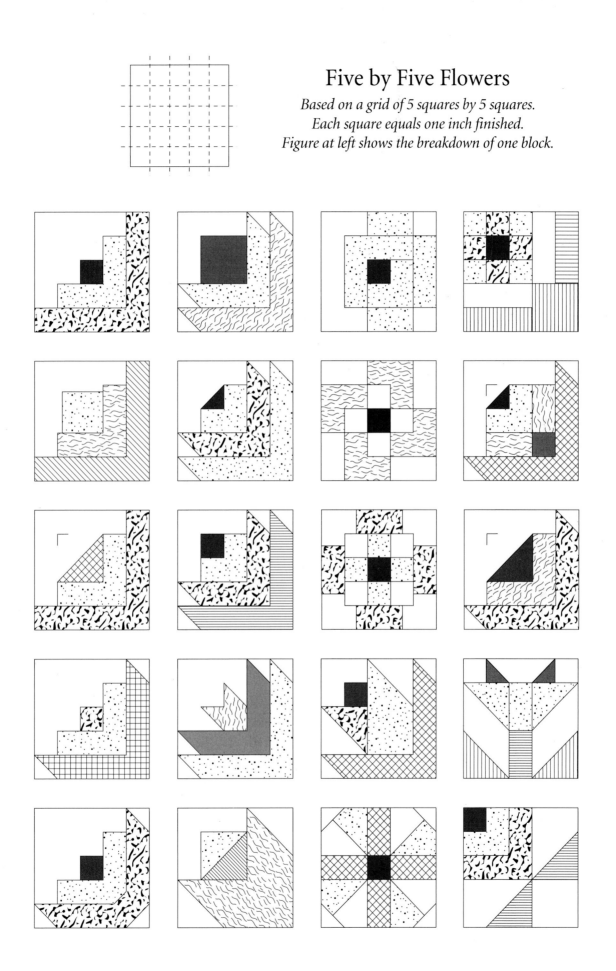

Lilies – Log Cabin Variations

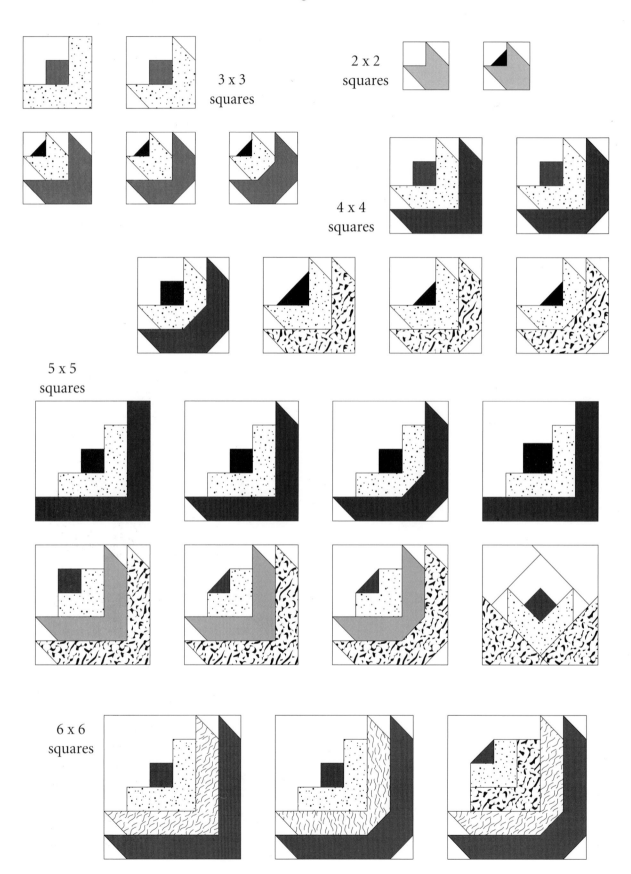

3 x 3
squares

2 x 2
squares

4 x 4
squares

5 x 5
squares

6 x 6
squares

Miscellaneous Flowers

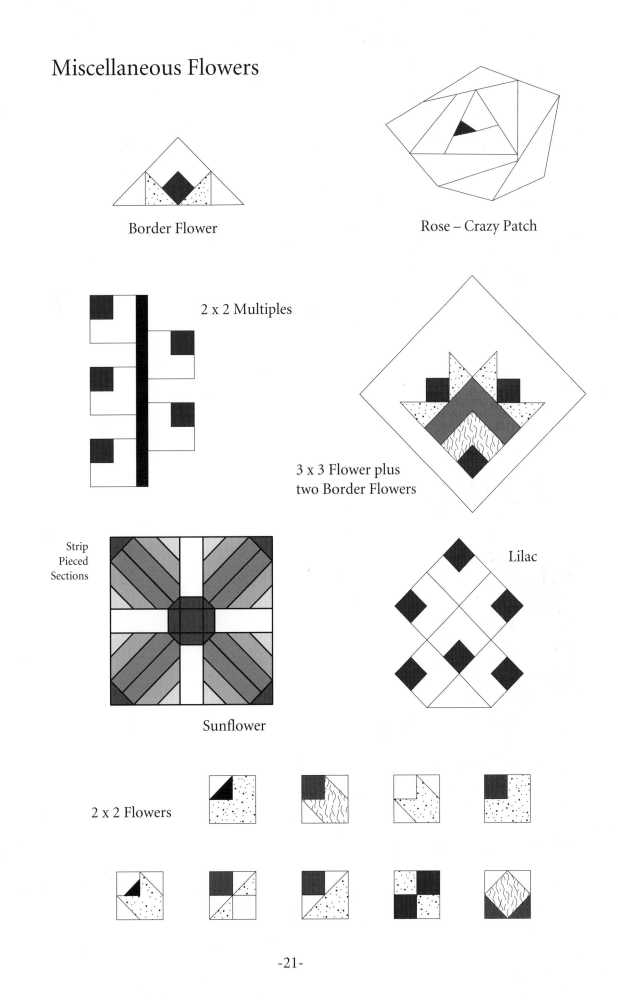

Border Flower

Rose – Crazy Patch

2 x 2 Multiples

3 x 3 Flower plus
two Border Flowers

Strip
Pieced
Sections

Sunflower

Lilac

2 x 2 Flowers

Leaf Ideas

The leaf variations shown on this page are used in
the diagrams throughout this book. Modify any example
of a leaf so that it fits the block size you are working with.

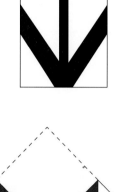

Simple leaf shapes.

 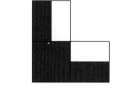 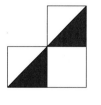 

More complex leaves.

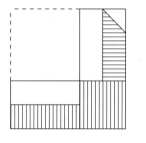 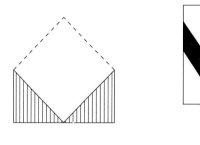

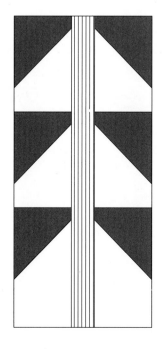 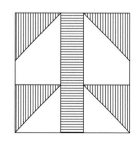

See *Five Large Flowers*, *Seven Large Flowers*, and *Sunflower By Day*.

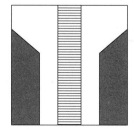

Borders

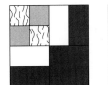

Borders can be as varied as your leaves, and as unique as your quilts. In these two examples I have alternated the position of the flower, and also the width between the blocks in the border.

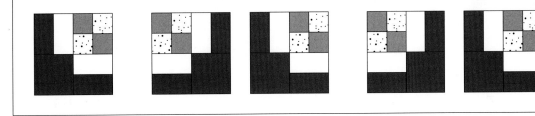

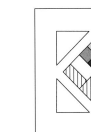 ---------- Seam Lines.

To make rectangle blocks – sew 4 half squares to the sides of the block. Trim. Sew strips on two sides if a wider border is wanted.

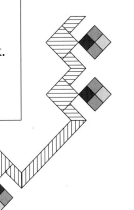

Vary the flower used or the angle placement.

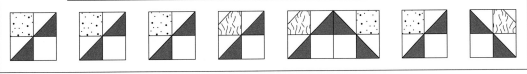

And Borders

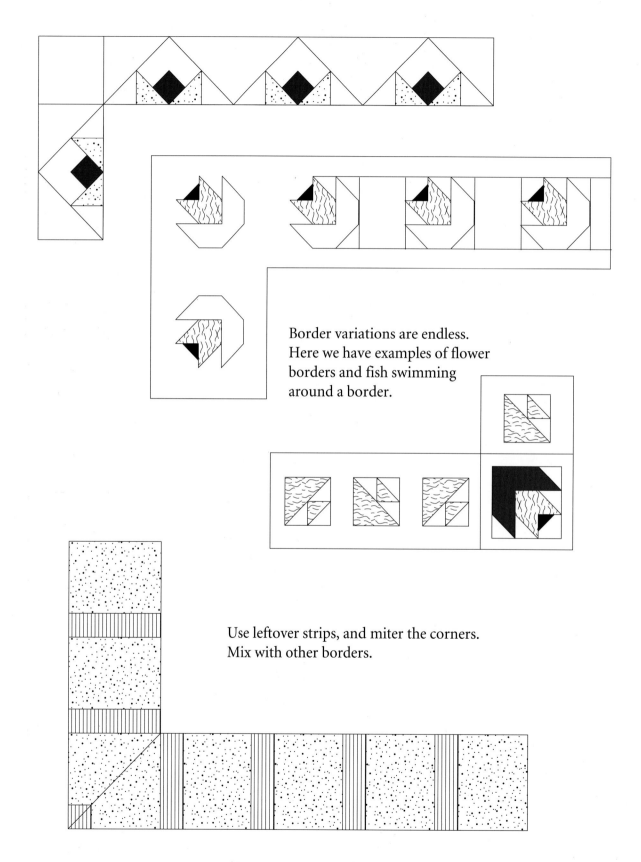

Border variations are endless.
Here we have examples of flower
borders and fish swimming
around a border.

Use leftover strips, and miter the corners.
Mix with other borders.

And More Borders

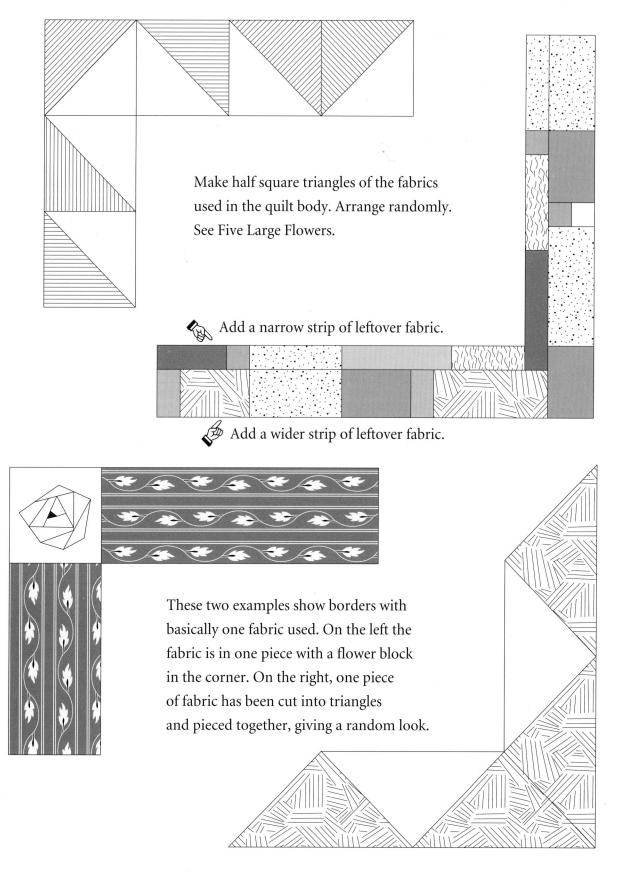

Make half square triangles of the fabrics used in the quilt body. Arrange randomly. See Five Large Flowers.

Add a narrow strip of leftover fabric.

Add a wider strip of leftover fabric.

These two examples show borders with basically one fabric used. On the left the fabric is in one piece with a flower block in the corner. On the right, one piece of fabric has been cut into triangles and pieced together, giving a random look.

Flower Worksheet

Permission given to copy this page for personal use only.
Suggestion: color, cut and paste your flower arrangement before cutting fabric!

CHAPTER THREE

Basic Construction Techniques

Half Square Triangle Cutting Chart

Method 1

▢ Starting Cut Squares	Unfinished ◣ Size	Finished ◣ Size
3½" x 3½"	3" x 3"	2½" x 2½"
4" x 4"	3½" x 3½"	3" x 3"
4½" x 4½"	4" x 4"	3½" x 3½"
5" x 5"	4½" x 4½"	4" x 4"
5½" x 5½"	5" x 5"	4½" x 4½"
6" x 6"	5½" x 5½"	5" x 5"
6½" x 6½"	6" x 6"	5½" x 5½"

Method 2

▬ Starting Cut Strips	Unfinished ◤ Size	Finished ◤ Size
1¼"	1½" x 1½"	1" x 1"
1½"	1¾" x 1¾"	1¼" x 1¼"
1¾"	2" x 2"	1½" x 1½"
1⅞"	2¼" x 2¼"	1¾" x 1¾"
2"	2½" x 2½"	2" x 2"
2¼"	2¾" x 2¾"	2¼" x 2¼"

Half Square Triangles

METHOD 1
for half square triangles over 2" finished

❖ Cut squares of fabric 1" larger than the finished size square you want.

❖ EXAMPLE – to make a 3" finished triangle square, cut a 4" square of background fabric, and a 4" square of another fabric.

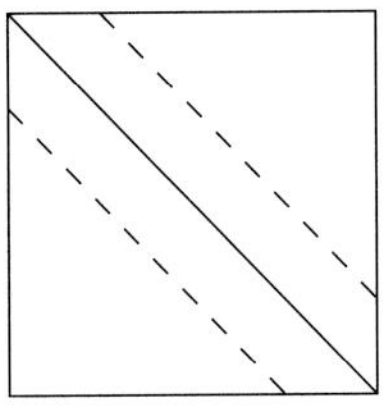

❖ Put two squares of fabric together, right sides facing. Draw a diagonal line on one square from corner to opposite corner. With the presser foot of your sewing machine against the line, stitch on both sides of this drawn line. *(figure 1)*

figure 1

❖ CUT on the drawn diagonal line. Open pieces – two triangle squares are made at the same time! These squares should measure 3½" x 3½" unfinished, and 3" x 3" when sewn into a quilt, assuming a ¼" seam allowance. *(figure 2)*

figure 2

Results
❖ Squares which are half triangles can be made fast and you can achieve a variety of half square combinations.

Bonus
❖ A half square triangle that is cut in half again is very useful. It will make a left and right leaf. *(figure 3)*

❖ The initial half square triangle you make for this needs to be big – at least 4" to 6".

❖ This is used to add leaves to a flower block that looks best on the diagonal.

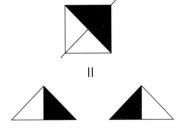

figure 3

Half Square Triangles

METHOD 2
for half square triangles 2" or smaller

❖ This is the technique used in the frog pattern for all sizes of triangle squares.

❖ PROBLEM – ALL EDGES ARE BIAS.

❖ CUT a strip of background fabric and a strip of print fabric of the same measurement, placing them right sides together.

❖ Sew BOTH long edges together using a ¼" seam allowance.

❖ Place the sewn strip set on a cutting board and, using a ruler as shown, move it along BOTH edges of the strip set and cut triangles.

❖ See the chart on page 29 for cut strip sizes needed to produce the desired half square triangles.

❖ Pick out stitches from the corner, then open the triangle piece to form a square.

❖ Carefully press from the top.

RESULTS
❖ The fastest way to make triangle squares. If they are small, the bias edge is not a problem.

BONUS
❖ From one set of sewn strips you can get many sizes of half square triangles. Different triangle measurements are achieved by simple movement of the ruler.

Using a ruler with a 45° angle, place the 45° line on the edge of the sewn strips and make a cut along the ruler edge.

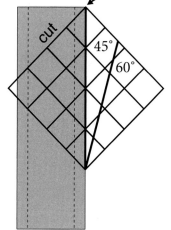

Discard this end scrap.

Again place the 45° line on the edge of the sewn strips and make a cut along the ruler edge.

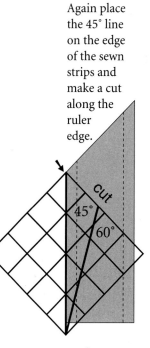

figure 4

Corner Triangles

figure 5

❖ Corner triangles are a great alternative to using half square triangles.

❖ They can be used to modify or add small changes to a block. For example – a 3 x 3 block becomes a daisy, and a log cabin block becomes a lily.

❖ A square of fabric is sewn diagonally in the corner of a block and pressed back toward a corner of the block to create a triangle. (*figure 5*)

figure 6

❖ EXAMPLE ONE – A 3 x 3 (a nine patch) made of one inch finished squares (1½" cut squares) looks more like a daisy when four 1½" squares of background fabric are placed on the four corners of the block and sewn in place diagonally. Press the created triangles into the corners – there will now be three layers of fabric here. Trim away the middle layer ONLY. The bottom layer is needed as a guide when sewing this block to other blocks. (*figure 6*)

❖ The four corners of the daisy will look rounded when the background strips are added to float the block.

figure 7

❖ EXAMPLE TWO – On a 3 x 3 log cabin block (made with 1½" strips) lay 1½" squares of background in the two corners covering the last two strips that were sewn. Sew these corner squares on diagonally and fold the triangle you have just created back toward the edge and trim away the middle layer. (*figure 7*)

❖ The points created gives the impression of flower petals or leaves.

- ❖ A GENERAL RULE: the corner squares are cut from the same width of strip used to construct the block on which you are working. (1½" corner squares are used on blocks made with 1½"strips.)

VARIATION ONE
Use a LARGER corner square.

- ❖ On the log cabin block (figure 7), if 1½" strips are used to create the lily block, then 1¾" cut squares will be used instead of the 1½" squares used in the previous example.

- ❖ By sewing on a larger square to create the corner triangle, the point you are creating is moved a little further in from the seam line. *(figure 8)*

figure 8

RESULTS
- ❖ Sharp points will not be lost into the seam allowance when blocks are sewn together.

VARIATION TWO
Use a SMALL corner square.

figure 9

- ❖ A flower made with a 1½" (or larger) starting square may look good with a small triangle in the corner. *(figure 9)*

- ❖ To do this, sew a 1¼" cut square diagonally to a 1½"or larger background square. Press the triangle back and trim away the middle layer. *(figure 9)*

figure 10

RESULTS
- ❖ A small design detail is added to a corner in the block. *(figure 10)*

- ❖ ANYTIME you see an angle off the corner of a block a corner square has been added to create the triangle – large or small.

Floating A Block

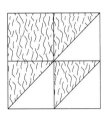

figure 11

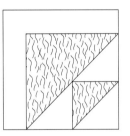

figure 12

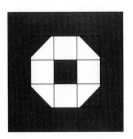

figure 13

Floating a block means adding background strips around a block so that the image in the block stands out.

EXAMPLE ONE

❖ A fish block is made of 4 squares sewn together. *(figure 11)*

❖ It does not look like a fish until at least two sides have background strips sewn onto the block. *(figure 12)*

❖ Now the image of the fish stands out.

EXAMPLE TWO

❖ Other designs may need strips sewn on all edges to make the image stand out.

❖ A daisy is a 3 x 3 block with four corner triangles added. *(See figure 6, page 32.)*

❖ The daisy image does not stand out until all four edges have background floating strips sewn onto the block. *(figure 13)*

Many of the quilt blocks shown in this book will look better if you FLOAT them before adding them to a quilt.

FLOAT quilt tops before adding borders. To do this, strips of any width of background fabric are added to the finished center. These floating strips separate the quilt top from the border. This design feature can add relief to the finished quilt where the center and the borders are both busy.

Trimming Up

❖ Trimming up the finished block is usually necessary because TEMPLATES are NOT used during construction.

❖ Some cuts made during construction (with scissors at the sewing machine) are not very accurate.

❖ If some blocks turn out too small, FLOAT these blocks and then trim these blocks to the same size as the other blocks.

How To Trim

❖ Determine the finished size of block needed. If the block will be 5" finished, then it will be trimmed to 5½", assuming a ¼" seam allowance.

❖ When determining trimming size, make sure you have allowed for a ¼" seam allowance on all four sides. The ends of any points must be at least ¼" in from any trimmed edge.

❖ Lay a large square ruler on top of the block to be trimmed. A diagonal line on the ruler is helpful in centering the ruler on the block.

❖ With a rotary cutter, cut or trim up two sides of the block.

❖ Lift the square ruler off the block and shift it. Now place the two edges of the ruler on the two uncut (or untrimmed) sides of the block.

❖ Line up diagonal line on the ruler the same as before.

❖ To cut a 5½" block, two 5½" lines on the ruler should line up with the two just cut sides of the block.

❖ With a rotary cutter, cut the remaining two sides.

❖ Blocks that float are the easiest to trim up.

RESULTS

Trimming up frees us from the use of templates, allows our work to be a little rough, and still end up with blocks the same size – so that the final construction of the quilt top is easy.

Leaves and Borders Worksheet

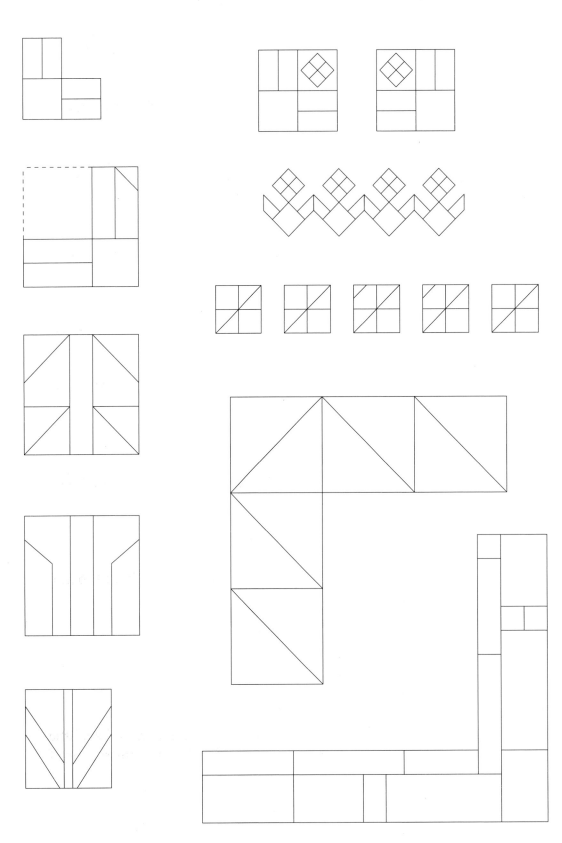

Permission given to copy this page for personal use only.

CHAPTER FOUR

PROJECT CONSTRUCTION

Crazy Patch

Crazy Patch is the random sewing together of odd shaped pieces to create a new piece of fabric.

In this book refer to the rose flower blocks, the large leaf pieces in *Sunflower by Day* and *Sunflower by Night*, and the complete border of *Moonlite Serenade*.

This method of block construction is time consuming. It could take well over an hour to make one rose block!

MAKING A ROSE – *Every rose block will be different.*

❖ Cut a starting shape. I like a triangle with three 60° angles and a 2" measurement on each side. Any size or shape could be used. *(figure 14)*

figure 14

❖ Cut large strips from the fabric you will be using to make the body of the rose. I cut 2" to 5" strips and then cut pieces from these as needed.

❖ Sew any cut piece to one edge of the starting triangle. Fold piece back.

❖ Using a ruler and a rotary cutter, cut one straight edge. This becomes the next edge that a strip will be sewn to. *(figure 15)*
  ❖ STEP 1 – Sew a cut piece to the straight edge.
  ❖ STEP 2 – Cut a new straight edge.
  ❖ Repeat Steps 1 and 2 until you like the shape of your rose.

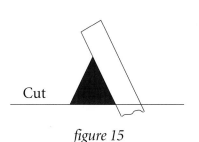

figure 15

❖ During these steps you will be cutting away some of the already sewn areas in order to create interesting angles in your rose.

DO NOT STOP HERE – Now take strips or pieces of background and continue around the rose following steps 1 and 2 until the piece is large enough to trim to a square or rectangle for use in a quilt.

The rose now floats in the background!

A Simple 4 x 4 Flower

❖ Choose three different fabrics to represent a flower, a leaf, and a background. Cut a 1½" strip of background fabric and a 1½" strip of leaf fabric.

❖ Put the strips together, right sides facing, and sew one long seam. Iron open. Chop off 2½" pieces from this sewn strip. Two cut pieces are needed for each flower block made.

❖ Cut a 2½" square of flower fabric and a 2½" square of leaf fabric for each block made.

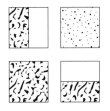

figure 16

❖ One flower block consists of the squares now cut. Lay out and sew together. *(figure 16)*

❖ The block will measure 4½"x 4½". Trim up if necessary. When sewn in with other blocks the finished measurement will be 4"x 4".

❖ You should be able to make eight of these flowers blocks from that one sewn strip set of background and leaf fabric.

VARIATION 1 – of a SIMPLE FLOWER

❖ Change the size of the strips you cut:
   ❖ Cut the background and leaf strips 1¼" wide.
   ❖ Stitch together and cut off 2" pieces.
   ❖ Cut the flower and leaf squares 2".
   ❖ Sew four pieces together as before.
   ❖ The flower block now measures 3½"x 3½".

VARIATION 2 – PUT BLOCK ON DIAGONAL

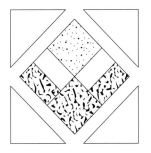

figure 17

❖ When the block is put on the diagonal, four triangles of background fabric will need to be added to create a square. *(figure 17)*

- ❖ Cut the triangles larger than needed, over-lapping them when sewing them onto the block. Trim the block down to the required size after it is finished.

VARIATION 3 – ADD CORNER TRIANGLES

- ❖ Corner triangles can be added to leaf ends so that they look pointed. *(figure 18)*

- ❖ Take the original block and add two squares of background fabric (1½"x 1½"), sew diagonally to the two leaf ends.

figure 18

- ❖ Press the triangle back and trim away the middle layer.

- ❖ This creates a more realistic looking flower.

VARIATION 4 – A DIFFERENT FLOWER

- ❖ Use a pieced flower instead of a cut square of flower fabric. For ideas, check the charts of flower blocks.

VARIATION 5 – VARY LEAF SIZE *(figure 19)*

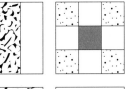

- ❖ Use the same leaf strip created in the original example.

- ❖ Create a pieced flower. We will use a 3 x 3 for this example.

figure 19

- ❖ Determine the size to cut the leaf and background strip by measuring the raw edge of the flower block. Slice off two pieces for leaves using this measurement.

- ❖ The cut square of leaf will remain 2½", the width of the sewn leaf strip set.

VARIATIONS of many of the flowers shown in the charts are possible, but it is up to you to discover how to create them!

Fish

A fish block is made of one square of fabric plus three squares of half triangles.

Any size of half square triangles can be used, but the three MUST be the same size. If you are working with leftover pieces, trim three to the same size.

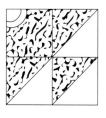

figure 20

❖ Cut a square of the fish fabric (not the background fabric) the same size as the half-square triangles.

❖ One fish block is made by sewing four squares together as shown. (figure 20)

❖ Match up the center seams. Trim up the block.

❖ This block needs to have floating strips sewn on to at least two sides to make the fish image stand out.

❖ This is a very useful little pattern to use in quilt tops along with frogs.

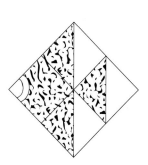

figure 21

❖ Large prints and bright colors are wonderful fabrics for fish.

❖ A nose section of the fish can be created by cutting a square of a large print in a selective way. Have a distinctive color or shape appear in the cut square and place this color or shape in the front position.

❖ Setting some of these blocks into a border so that it looks like the fish are swimming around the edge add a nice light touch to any quilt.

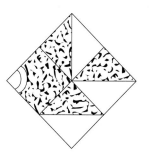

figure 22

❖ The fish block looks more like a fish image when it is set diagonally in a quilt. (figure 21)

❖ An alternative layout is given for the the four squares that make up the fish block. (figure 22)

Oriental Fish Quilt

❖ The finished size of this quilt is 39" x 50" and includes a 4" border. Small amounts of seven wild prints were used for the fish; 1½ yards of background fabric were used; and ¾ yards of border fabric were used.

❖ Three sizes of half square triangles are needed to make the fish . Cut 3" half square triangles for the large fish, 2½" half square triangles for the medium fish, and 2" half square triangles for the small fish. Each fish needs three half square triangles and one square, the same size, cut from fish fabric.

❖ Make seven large fish; seventeen medium fish; and fourteen small fish.

❖ Create seven large blocks consisting of one large, one medium, and two small fish, and use 1½" strips of background fabric to space fish in the block.

❖ Add 1½"cut strips to two sides of the large block. *(figure 23)*

❖ Trim the seven large blocks to the same size.

❖ Sew 1½" background strips to two edges of the remaining ten medium size fish so as to float the fish image in the block.

❖ Lay out the blocks as shown. *(figure 24)*. Cut twenty large triangles of background fabric and fill in around the edges.

❖ Sew together in diagonal rows including the edge triangles as part of the row. Square up the quilt and add borders. Add larger borders if you would like a bigger quilt.

❖ This size is perfect for a baby quilt.

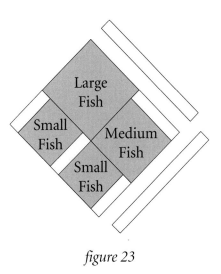

figure 23

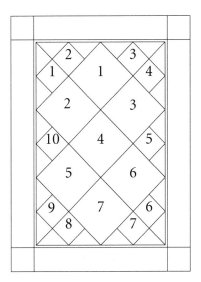

figure 24

FROG

The most difficult pattern to make in this book is the frog block. Once you make one, though, the results are worth it. The instructions that follow will make one frog.

There is a chart on page 49 which shows the various sizes of strips to cut for the various sizes of frogs you may want to make. The following instructions will give you the most common size frog block that I use in my patterns (line 3 on the chart.)

FROG INSTRUCTIONS – STEP BY STEP

❖ Choose a background fabric and a frog fabric. From the background fabric cut one 2¼" strip and two 1¾" strips. From the frog fabric cut one 2¼" strip and one 1¾" strip.

❖ Take both of the 2¼" strips and cut a 4½" piece off each one.

❖ Put two 2¼" x 4½" pieces together (right sides facing) and sew a seam along one 2¼" edge. Open and press with a warm iron. Set this piece aside for later use. The middle section is now complete.

❖ We will now make two side sections. One is the reverse of the other.

❖ Using Method 2 for constructing half square triangles, take one 1¾" strip of background and one 1¾" strip of frog fabric. Line up with right sides together and sew both long edges together.

❖ Iron this piece and lay out on a cutting board.

❖ See page 29 – Half Square Triangles – Method 2.

❖ Move the ruler along the strip and cut the whole strip into triangles which will then open into half square triangles after you have removed a couple of stitches from the corner.

❖ Six half square triangles are needed for each frog.

❖ Finger press open or iron open from the top.

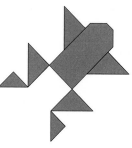

❖ If you lay six half square triangles on the pattern picture of the frog, you will see that the next step is to add some background extension pieces in two places for each side. To do this you will:

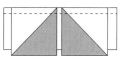

figure 25

❖ **STEP 1.** Take the remaining cut 1¾" background strip. Lay the strip down and place a half square triangle on it so that a background (or extension) piece will be sewn to the half square triangle. Immediately lay the half square triangle from the opposite side of the frog onto the strip to sew on its background extension piece at the same time. The second piece placed on the strip will look like the mirror image of the first in this placement. *(figure 25 unfinished and 25.1 finished)*

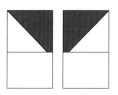

figure 25.1

❖ **STEP 2.** Cut these two pieces apart, then sew a half square triangle on to the extension piece. The frog fabric in each half square triangle must be in the same position for both half square triangles. *(figure 26 unfinished and 26.1 finished)*

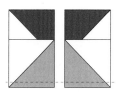

figure 26

❖ Working in pairs, sewing one side and then the other side will cause fewer headaches!

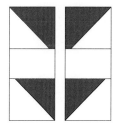

figure 26.1

❖ **STEP 3.** The most difficult part is this next step – to add on an extension piece and make the foot (another half square triangle) smaller at the same time. On the full size pattern sheet you can see where the piece is added. You need to trim ½" off the half-square triangle for each foot. *(figure 27 unfinished and 27.1 finished)*

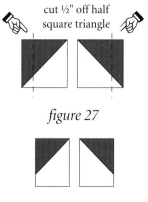

cut ½" off half square triangle

figure 27

figure 27.1

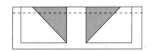

figure 28

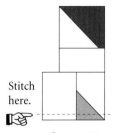

figure 28.1

Stitch
here.

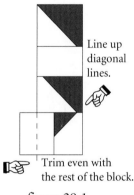

figure 29

Line up
diagonal
lines.

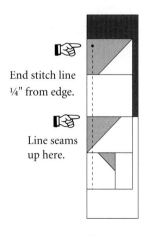

Trim even with
the rest of the block.

figure 29.1

End stitch line
¼" from edge.

Line seams
up here.

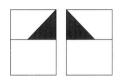

figure 30

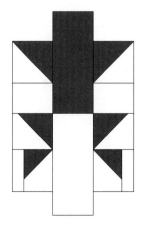

figure 31

❖ Place these trimmed pieces on the background strip so that a piece of the background strip will be sewn to the TRIMMED edge of both half square triangles. Cut apart. *(figure 28 unfinished and 28.1 finished)*

❖ Make the reverse side section at the same time.

❖ Iron the two side sections.

❖ **Step 4.** Sew this last piece created to the side sections from step two, lining up the two diagonal seams when they are on top of each other. *(figure 29 unfinished and 29.1 finished)*

FINAL ASSEMBLY

❖ You will now attach both completed side sections to the middle section previously made. There is only one seam to match up here. *(figure 30 unfinished and 31 finished)*

❖ Stop sewing at the top of each side section so that the seam allowance is free. If you do sew to the very end of the row you will later have to pick out three or four stitches.

❖ Iron flat.

- ❖ To complete the head, use the 2¼" strip of background left from making the middle section. If the frog blocks are to go into a specific pattern, I do not complete the head at this time because a larger background piece may be needed.

- ❖ Lay the background strip on the frog block, right sides together, and start sewing from the block edge. Stop sewing before you reach the middle section. *(figure 32)*

- ❖ The head piece must be loose and not caught in any stitches so that it can be pulled to the front of the block and laid over the top of the strip just sewn. *(figure 33)*

- ❖ Trim the head piece if necessary, then fold and shape as desired. Hand sew into place onto the strip underneath. *(figure 34)*

- ❖ Trimming up the block will be necessary. At this point it is a rectangular block. *(figure 35)*

- ❖ To make a square block, sew strips to two sides of the block and trim again. Squares are easier to put into quilts than rectangles.

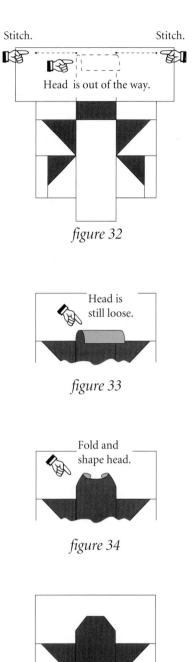

Stitch.   Stitch.

Head is out of the way.

figure 32

Head is still loose.

figure 33

Fold and shape head.

figure 34

figure 35

WHY MAKE FROG QUILTS?

Everyone seems to love frogs.

Lack of frogs is becoming a concern in the environment.

They're unfrogettable?

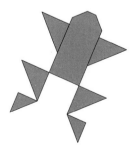

Frog

Unfinished actual size block when using 2¼ " and 1¾ " strips.

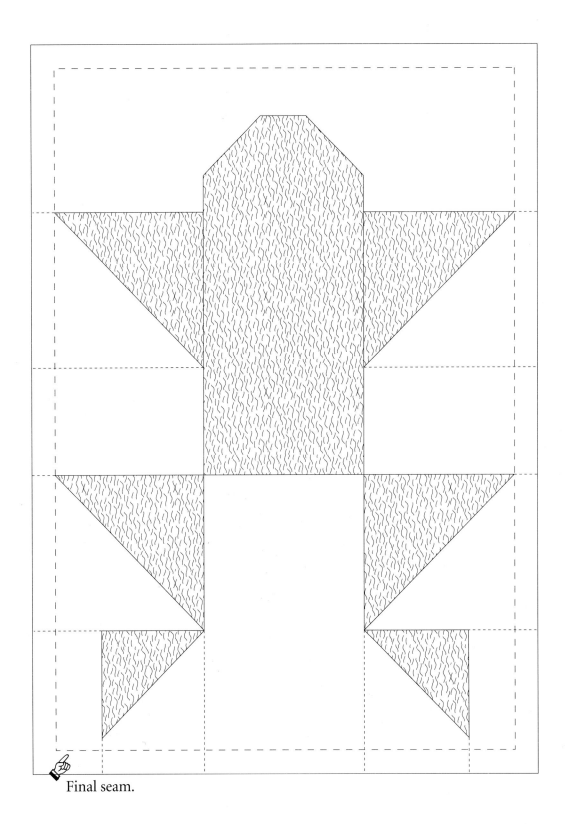

Final seam.

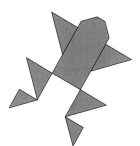

Frog
Chart of Sizes

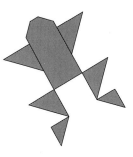

Cut Strips 1 Background 1 Frog	Middle Section Piece Size	Cut Strips 2 Background 1 Frog	Unfinished ◣	Trim Block this size or larger
1¾"	1¾" x 3½"	1¼"	1½"	3¾" x 5½"
2"	2" x 4"	1½"	1¾"	4½" x 6½"
2¼"	2¼" x 4½"	1¾"	2"	5½" x 7"
2½"	2½" x 5¼"	2"	2½"	6½" x 9"
3"	3" x 6"	2¼"	2¾"	7" x 9½"

◣ Half-square triangles are made using Method 2.

All the written instructions given in this book are for the third size listed above. It has been highlighted for easy reference. Please note that these sizes are for the cut sizes.

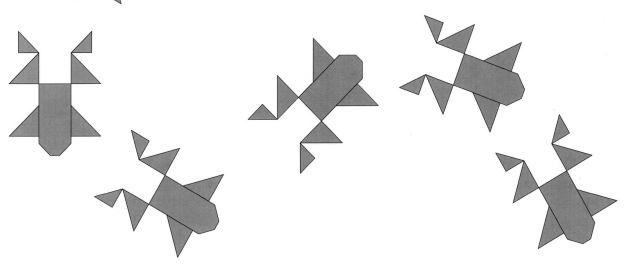

Instructions for a 5 x 10 Daisy

figure 36

figure 37

figure 38

figure 39

figure 40

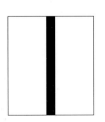

figure 41

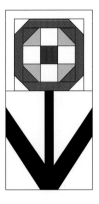

❖ Unless otherwise stated, cut fabric for all strips 1½". I chose a variety of purple fabrics for these in my quilt *A Field of Daisies.*

❖ Make a 3 x 3 block *(figure 36)* and then add 4 corner triangles *(figure 37)* of the fabric that will surround the flower.

❖ Cut a 1" strip of the corner fabric and sew on all four sides of the 3 x 3 block. *(figure 38)*

❖ Cut four 1" squares of background and add corner triangles. *(figure 39)*

❖ Cut 1½" strips of background and sew to 3 sides of this block *(figure 40)*. Set aside.

❖ Cut 2¾" strips for background, 1" strips for stem and sew a set of background-stem-background *(figure 41)*. Cut this strip set into 6½" segments.

❖ Sew a stem segment (fig. 41) to the flower top (fig. 40) piece on the side where there is no background strip. This side is the bottom of the daisy block. Set aside.

❖ Cut a strip of green leaf fabric 2½" wide. Lay this strip right sides together and stitch to the set of background-stem-background at an angle to create a leaf look, crossing the stem at least ½" from the bottom. Many looks are possible depending on the angle created with the leaf strip. *(figure 42)*

figure 42

❖ Trim away the excess part of the block and set aside. Press leaf. *(figure 43)*

❖ Retrieve the excess portion of the stem set and stitch to the other side, right sides together, of the leaf strip. *(figure 44)*. Press. Cut away excess fabric to square up the block. *(figure 45)*

figure 43

❖ Add leaf to the other side of stem *(figure 46)* following the steps shown for figure 42 through 45.

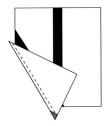

❖ Trim the block to 5½" x 10½". I mix these purple daisies in quilts with 5½" x 5½" white daisy blocks.

figure 44

❖ Your finished block will look like this. *(figure 47)*

figure 45

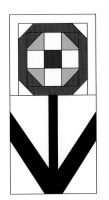

figure 47

figure 46

Project Diary

Beginning Name of Project _____

Date Project Started _____

Date Project Finished _____

Current Events during project construction _____

_____

_____

Size of Quilt _____

Quilt Made for _____

Final Name of Quilt _____

Fabrics Used (paste sample pieces here):

IS MAN SUPERIOR?
62" x 63"
The first quilt to use the frog.
This quilt is asking does man
have the right to overpower the
land, the seas and the skies.

FROG, FISH, LILIES
28" x 33"
Smaller poster size quilts
are fun and fast to make.
They are also a good place
to experiment with new
color combinations.

COMPLEX FLOWER SAMPLER

28" x 35"

Before I planned patterns on graph paper I would sew many miscellaneous flowers together in this complicated way. I now plan ahead on graph paper to make the sewing much simpler.

FROGS, FISH, LILIES

24" x 24"

The first challenge I ever did and it won first prize in a Canadian competition. The challenge fabrics were blue, aqua & white. I added orange & red to warm up the piece. In the collection of Eunice McLeod.

A WREATH OF LILIES

31" x 31"

A Christmas theme that could be used all year. Two sizes of lily make the wreath. The wreath is set on the diagonal in this sample.

SUNFLOWER BY DAY
24" x 39"
This pattern was created
so that I could use the two
sunflower border fabrics.
A quick piece to make.

SUNFLOWER BY NIGHT
24" x 39"

PLAYING WITH BATIKS
24" x 36"
The desire to use some batik
fabrics and bright pinks
made this piece happen.

WHIMSICAL FROGS
45" x 55"
A quick project made to use a strip of braid 7" wide for a humorous look.

A MOONLIGHT SERENADE
45" x 50"
This is the only piece made with lamés and party fabrics. There are six sizes of frogs and the effect is wonderful. A crazy patch border of party fabrics creates the correct mood to complete this wall hanging. The lamés are lined up so that it looks like moonlight crossing the quilt.

FIELD OF DAISIES
49" x 53"
*Simple white daisies and more
complicated purple daisies let me play
with opposites on the color wheel.*

PINK FROG, FISH & LILY
23" x 23"
*A simple piece to make with no
diagonal set. Many blocks this size
could be made for a larger piece.*

ORIENTAL FISH
40" x 52"
Many interesting fabrics
are used to create three
sizes of fish. This would
make a great baby quilt.

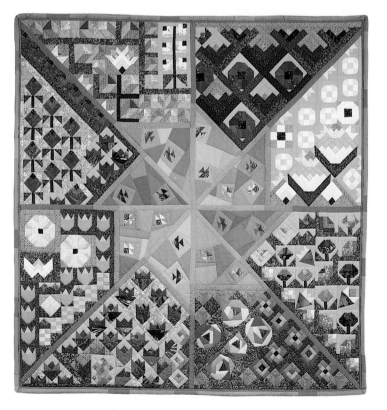

EIGHT GARDENS
64" x 63"
Because of creating
thirty-three varieties of
flowers for this quilt, I
decided to write this
book. The fish are set
crazy patch into the
water sections.

LEFTOVERS
50" x 74"
A big piece because I had lots of leftover flowers. Sewing rows together is fairly simple construction. A wild border print completes the look.

THE POND
44" x 52"
This quilt was the second quilt I made with frogs – there were eight leftover from my first project. Everything else was created to go with the frogs.

A FROG AND FISH SET
22" x 28" each
Some frog and fish blocks were made and then set with simple blocks
made like the blocks shown in the book "One of a Kind Quilts."

 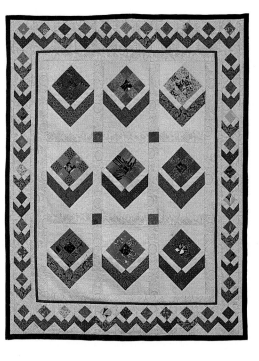

GEOMETRIC FLOWER I
33" x 42"
A simple flower is made and repeated
many times to create a block. A smaller
version is used for the border.

GEOMETRIC FLOWER II
33" x 42"
This is a variation of the simple flower
used in version I – but every flower is
used on the diagonal. A much more
complicated piece to make .

FIVE RED FLOWERS
40" x 45"
Any flower – or five different flowers could be used in this pattern. In the border, keep the darker fabrics to the outside edge.

PINK AND BLUE CHALLENGE
24" x 33"
A frog, fish and flower piece that is a good balanced design. The fish border adds movement around the outside.

PASTEL GARDENS

51" x 53"

I like using many background fabrics instead of one, for a more interesting look. This is a small pattern made four times and sewn together to create a medallion look.

SMALL PASTEL GARDENS

30" x 32"

Many of the flower patterns look best when used in a diagonal set.

WINDOW GARDENS
50" x 54"
An attic window set for
various samples of flowers is
always effective.

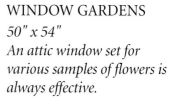

WINE FROGS & FLOWERS
29" x 34"
Another poster size quilt. In this one,
three wine background fabrics were
used plus another one for the border.
In the collection of Jean Thompson.

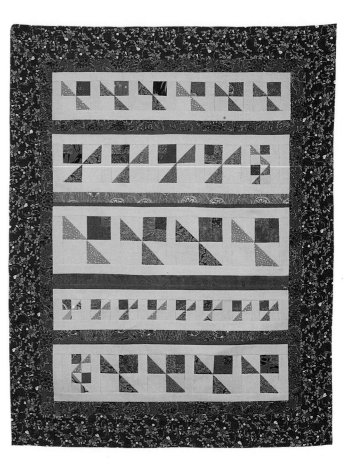

ONE FLOWER – MANY SIZES
35" x 44"
A variation of a simple flower made
many sizes and set in rows. Any
flower could be used this way.

YELLOW ROSES
42" x 43"
One flower made in different sizes.
The opposite colors of yellow and
purple were used.

CHAPTER FIVE

Quilt Designs

Geometric Flowers

This quilt could be made using any one of the four different flower block variations and two leaf variations shown. Choose borders from the border section.

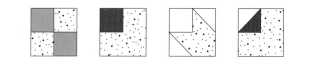

A Field of Purple & White Daisies

50" x 60"

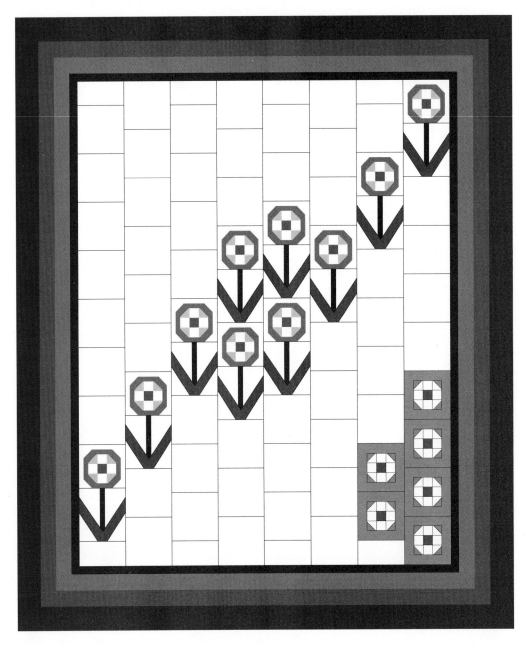

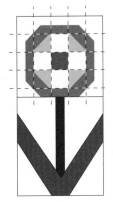 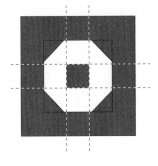 The daisy block is enlarged and shown here with a grid overlay. The scale of the grid is 1 square = 1 inch.

Purple and White Daisies
Poster Size Quilts

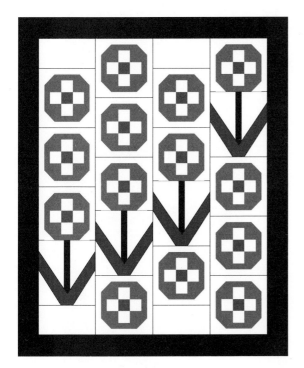

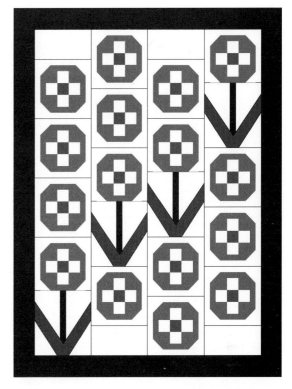

20" x 25" plus Border

20" x 27 " plus Border

Be creative with your background
fabrics and try: Plains or Prints
Bright Colors
Pastel Colors
Red & Black

Again, this
daisy has been
enlarged to
show the block
break down.
The scale is
1 square = 1 inch.

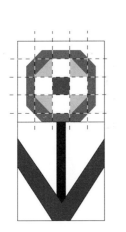

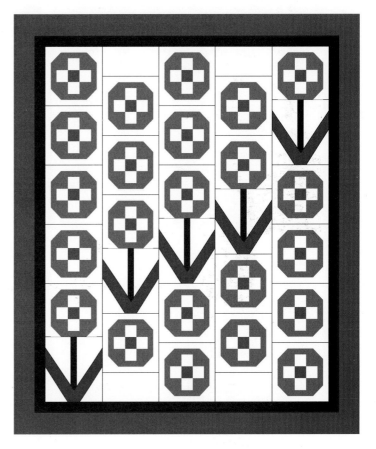

25" x 30" plus Border

Five Large Flowers

Starting square is a half square triangle.

Flower 6 x 6

Sky 6 x 6

2 x 2

4 x 4

Leaf 2 x 2

Border 5 x 5

Finished square sizes are given.

Seven Large Flowers

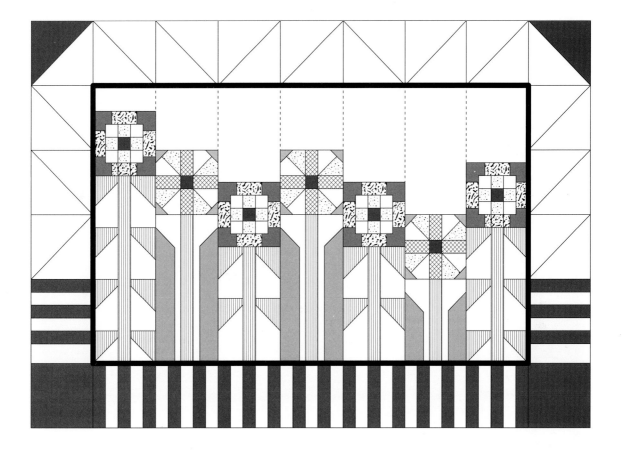

	SIZE	MAKE
Flower Use any one or many.	5 x 5	7
Leaf	2 x 2	22
Border Use various greens, aquas, purples.	4 x 4 ◣	15
	4 x 1"	strips
	4 x 4	2

Use one or many fabrics for background sky.

All Over Flower

Make any size – even bed size. This design consists of 6 x 6 flowers.
For the diagram above, I chose a flower from the 4 x 4 section and
enlarged to the 6 x 6 size. Leaves are added last as corner triangles.
The sections of the inside border consist of flower fabrics, and the
outside sections are from the leaf fabric.

A Rose Is A Rose Is A Rose
30" x 34"

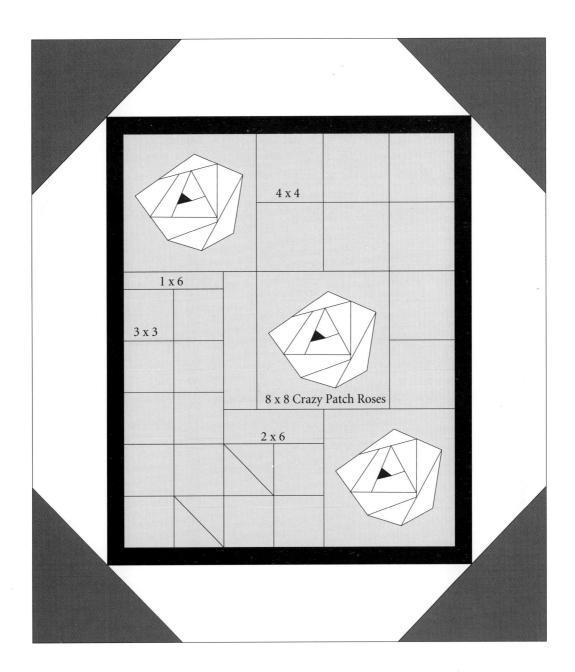

Use rose fabrics in the corners! Background fabrics can be squares, half square triangles, or other flower blocks. In the layout above, block sizes have been suggested.

Sunflower By Day – Sunflower By Night

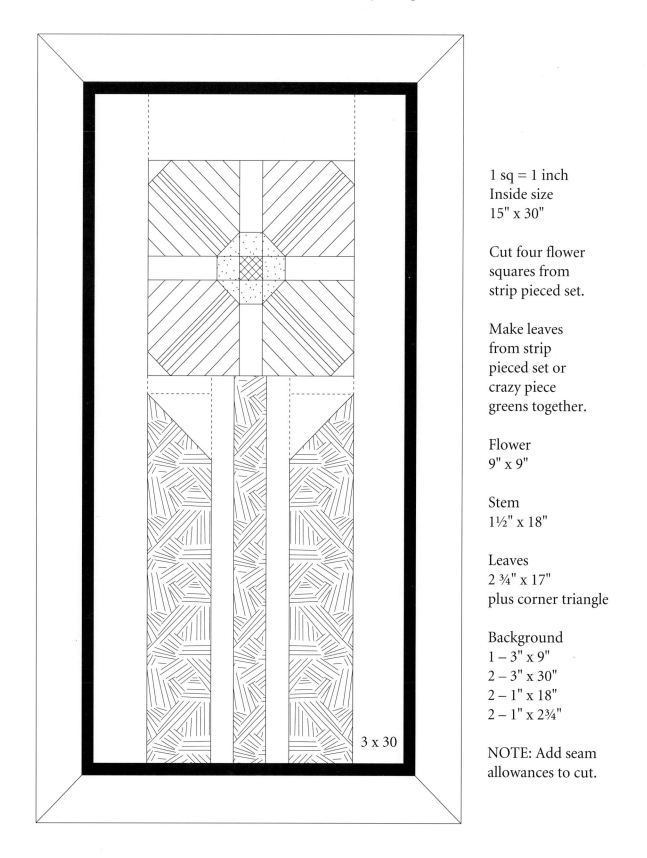

3 x 30

1 sq = 1 inch
Inside size
15" x 30"

Cut four flower
squares from
strip pieced set.

Make leaves
from strip
pieced set or
crazy piece
greens together.

Flower
9" x 9"

Stem
1½" x 18"

Leaves
2 ¾" x 17"
plus corner triangle

Background
1 – 3" x 9"
2 – 3" x 30"
2 – 1" x 18"
2 – 1" x 2¾"

NOTE: Add seam
allowances to cut.

Pastel Gardens

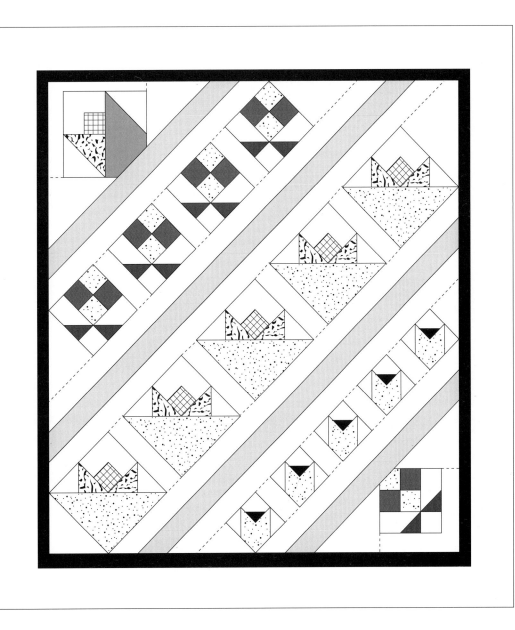

Use flower blocks that look good on
the diagonal. Number of blocks needed:

4 x 4 Flowers – 6 Blocks

3 x 3 Flowers – 5 Blocks

2 x 2 Flowers – 5 Blocks

Fill in with 1" (1½" cut) strips and some background triangles.
For a larger quilt, make blocks for four small quilts. See the
photo on page 62.

Paths Between Gardens
32"x 35"

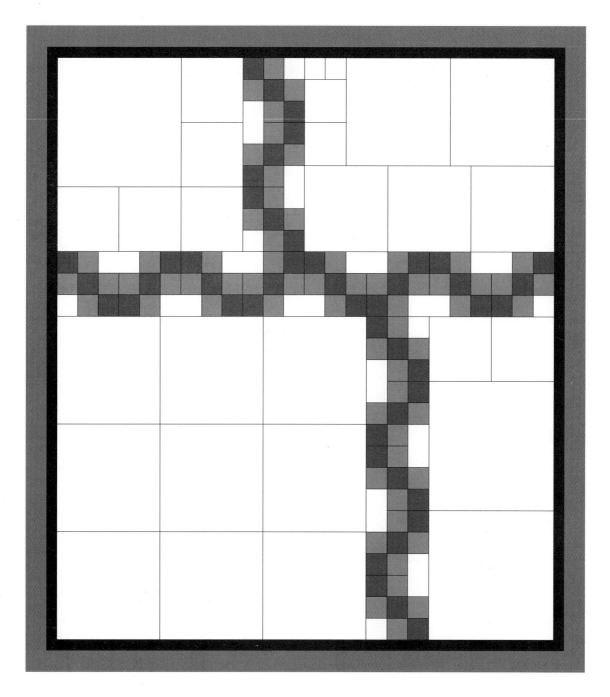

 3 x 3 blocks of black, grey and green make the garden paths.
1 square - 1 inch.

Fill in with flower blocks and some background fabric blocks.
The quilt shown above contains 1 x 1, 2 x 2, 3 x 3, 4 x 4, 5 x 5, and 6 x 6 blocks.

Sampler #1
For blocks that look best on the diagonal.

Blocks Needed:
2 x 2 Flowers - 2" x 2" - 14 Blocks
3 x 3 Flowers - 3" x 3" - 9 Blocks
4 x 4 Flowers - 4" x 4" - 10 Blocks

27" x 33" plus borders
Fill in with 1" (1½" cut)
background strips and
some triangles.

Sampler #2

25" x 29" plus borders

2 x 2 Flowers or Fish - 2" x 2" -   6 Blocks
3 x 3 Flowers or Fish - 3" x 3" - 17 Blocks
4 x 4 Flowers or Fish - 4" x 4" -   1 Block

Sampler #3

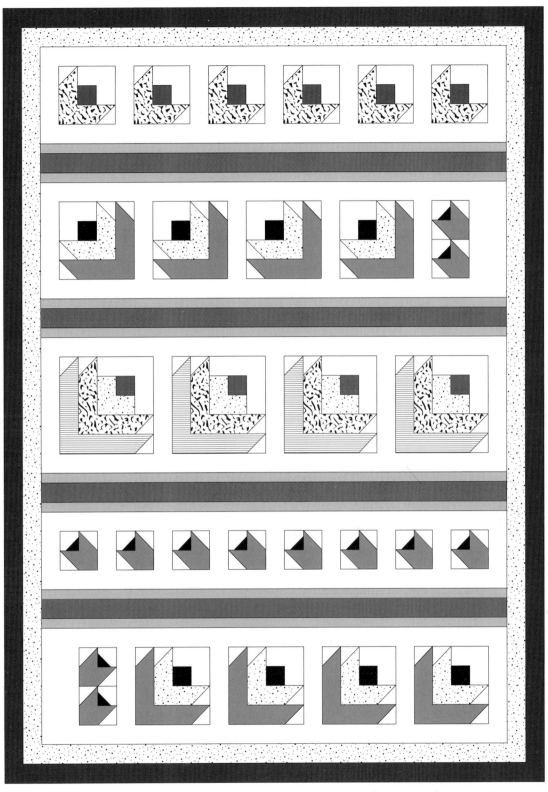

One flower made many sizes:

2 x 2 Flowers - 12 Blocks   4 x 4 Flowers - 8 Blocks
3 x 3 Flowers -   6 Blocks   5 x 5 Flowers - 4 Blocks

Frog Fish & Lilies

28"x 32"

	CUT	MAKE
Frogs	2¼" & 1¾" strips	3
Lilies	1½" strips	1 - 6 x 6
		1 - 5 x 5
		3 - 4 x 4
Fish	1½" squares	7
Border	3" strips	

To fill in the background, cut large squares on the diagonal and 1½" and 2½" strips.

Frog, Fish & Lily
A Fast Project
27" x 27"

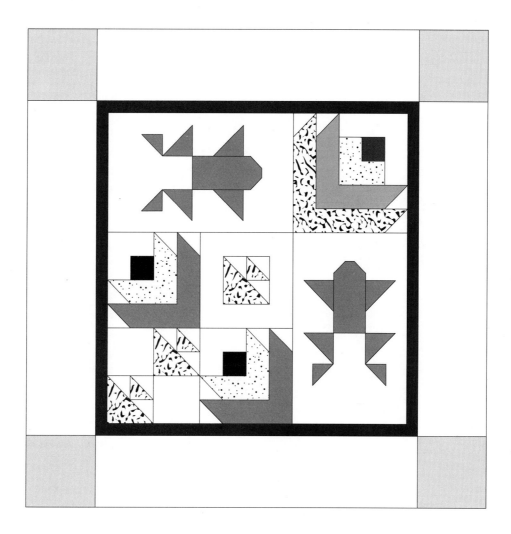

		CUT	Finished Block Sizes
Frog		1¾" strips	2 - 5 x 8
		2¼" strips	
		2½" under head	
Lilies		1½" strips	1 - 5 x 5 block
			2 - 4 x 4 blocks
Fish		1½" squares	3 - 2 x 2
Border		3½" of frog or fish fabric	

A Wreath of Lilies

This was constructed as a 24" x 24" center panel.

After completing the center panel you may add borders or put the center panel on the diagonal and add four 6 x 6 lily blocks at the corners. These two suggestions are shown on the following page.

	CUT	MAKE
Lilies	1½" strips	4 - 6 x 6
		16 - 4 x 4
Background	4½" x 4½"	4
	2½" x 6½"	4
	2½" x 8½"	4

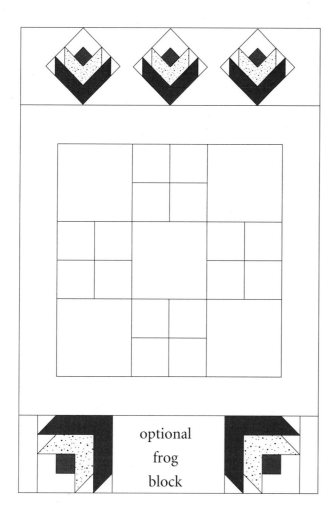

Wreath of Lilies

Add borders to center panel.

optional
frog
block

Wreath of Lilies

*Put center panel on
diagonal and add four
6 x 6 lily blocks at corners.*

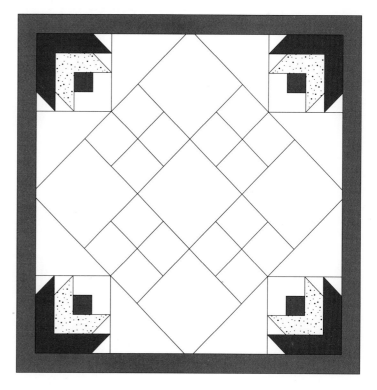

A Small Pond
24" x 24"

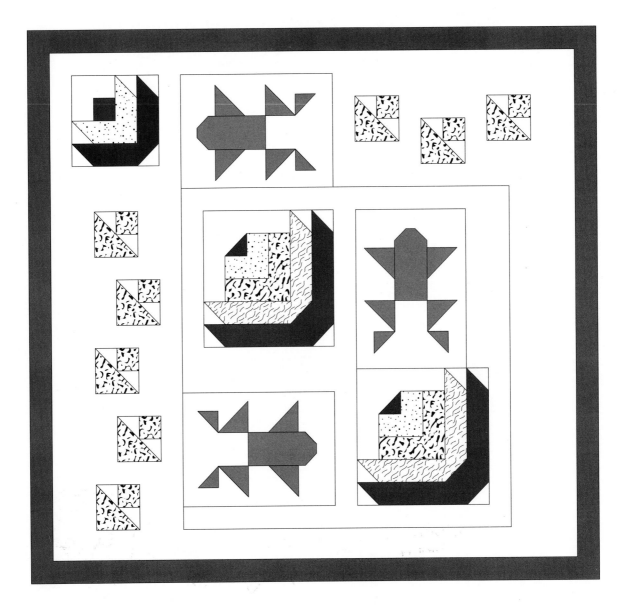

	MAKE
Frogs	3 - 5 x 7
Lilies	2 - 6 x 6
	1 - 4 x 4
Fish	8 - 2 x 2

The Pond
18" x 26" plus borders

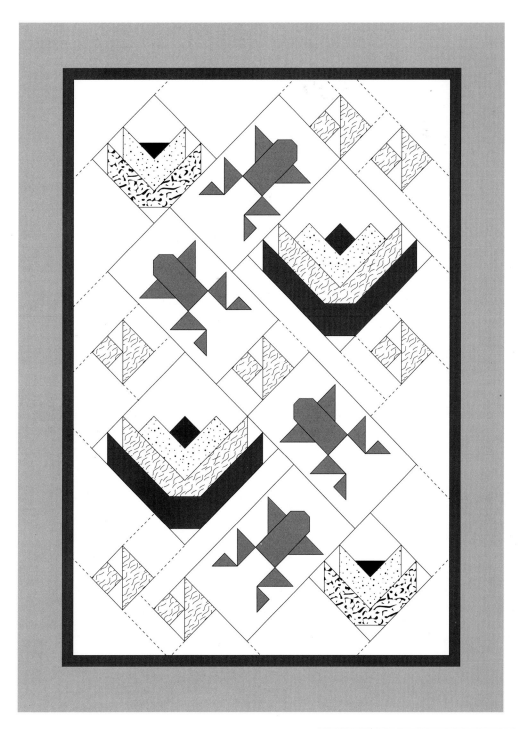

A well balanced quilt.

	SIZE	MAKE
Frog	4 x 7	4
Lilies	6 x 6	2
	4 x 4	2
Fish	2 x 2	7

The Lily Pond
30" x 35"

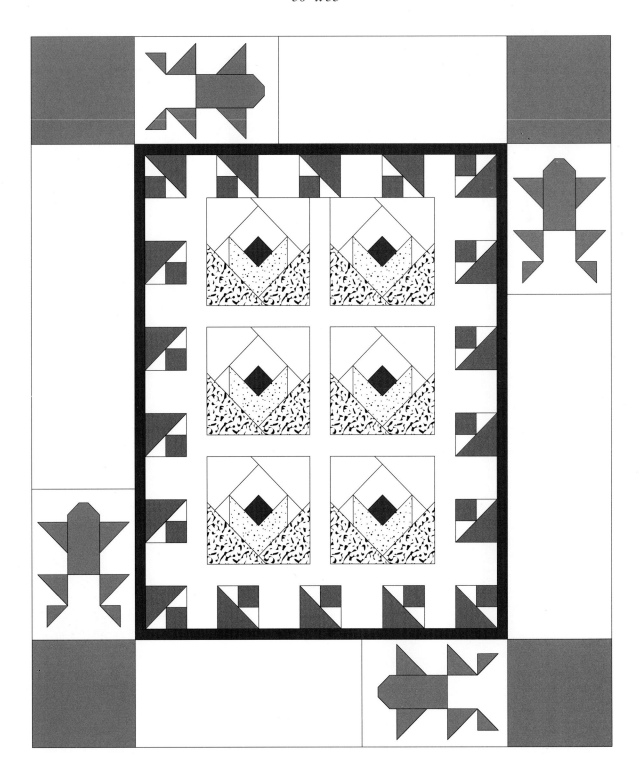

Make six or ten 5 x 5 lily blocks and eighteen 2 x 2 fish blocks. Vary the position of the fish. In the corners use lily blocks or squares of lily fabric. 5 x 7 frog blocks in the border are optional.

Flowers and Fish
28" x 33"

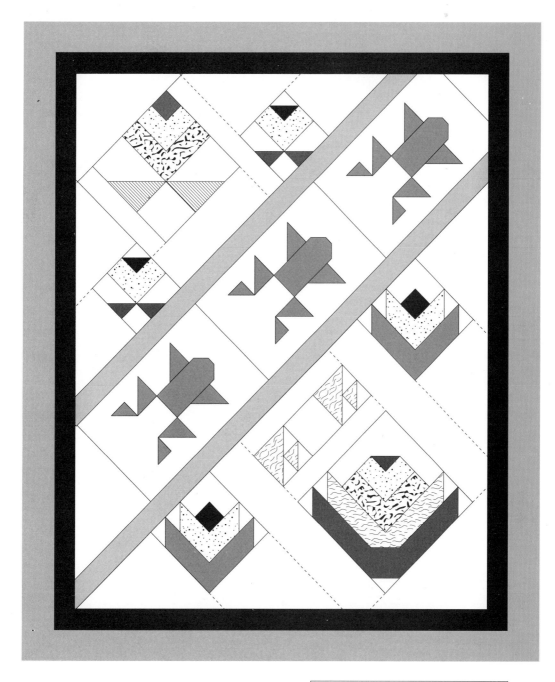

Three different background fabrics.

	Finished Size
Frogs	3 - 5 x 8
Lilies	1 - 6 x 6
	1 - 5 x 5
	2 - 4 x 4
	2 - 3 x 3
Fish	2 - 2 x 2
Border	4"

24" Challenge

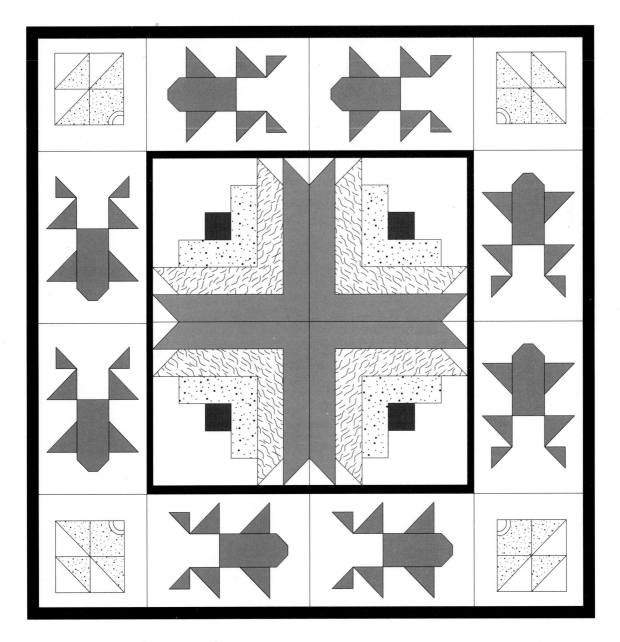

	CUT	Finished Block Size
Lily	1½" strips	6 x 6
Frog Body	2¼" strips	5 x 7
◣	1¾" strips	
Under Head	2½" strips	
Fish	2" x 2" ◣	3 x 3

You Have To Kiss A Lot Of Frogs Before You Find A Prince

Make 16 frog blocks. Trim to 5½" x 8½" (unfinished), then sew a strip to one side of each block. This strip is indicated in the layout above by a dotted line. Put random diamonds in the border. This quilt will be 24" x 34" before borders.

Project Worksheet

Project Worksheet

Project Worksheet

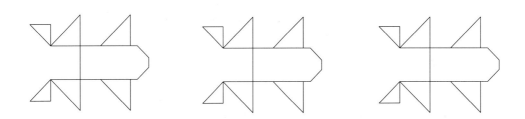

Project Worshet

Bibliography

Hargrave, Harriet. *Heirloom Machine Quilting.* Westminster, CA: Burdett Publications, 1987.

Hopkins, Mary Ellen. *It's Okay If You Sit On My Quilt Book.* Santa Monica, CA: ME Publications, 1989.

Hopkins, Mary Ellen. *Baker's Dozen Doubled.* Santa Monica, CA: ME Publications, 1988.

Hopkins, Judy. *One Of A Kind Quilts.* Bothell, WA: That Patchwork Place, 1989.

LaBranche, Carol. *Patchwork Pictures.* Pittstown, NJ: The Main Street Press, Inc., 1985.

Leone, Diane. *Attic Windows.* Santa Clara, CA: Leone Publications, 1989.

McMorris, Penny & Michael Kyle. *The Art Quilt.* San Francisco: The Quilt Digest Press, 1986.

Mosey, Caron L. *America's Pictoral Quilts.* Paducah, KY: The American Quilter's Society, 1985.

Schlotzhauer, Joyce M. *The Curved Two-Patch System.* McLean, VA: EPM Publications, Inc., 1982.

Stevens, Peter S. *Handbook of Regular Patterns.* MIT Press, 1984.

About The Author

Camille Remme has made a name for herself in Canada as a quiltmaker since 1984, and teacher since 1987. She was featured in *Ladies Circle Patchwork Quilts*, January, 1989, in an article entitled *Diverse Designs by Camille.*

Camille did not consider herself very creative because she could not draw. Her love of mathematics combined with the use of graph paper has led her down a different path to creativity – quilting has proved to be the perfect medium. Combine this creativity with excellent sewing skills and a keen color sense, and Camille thrives on making quilts by machine using contemporary techniques.